Wreath—The First Week of Advent

If you want your Advent wreath to look like the one in church, color three candles purple and one rose or pink. Or use your favorite colors.

people of Israel

king

slavery

heal the sick

set the people free

Advent

Jesus

Christmas

The Story of Advent and Christmas

A long time ago, the  were waiting for a  to be born. This  would save the  from . The  would  and  from their enemies. The  waited a very long time for their good  to be born.

During the four weeks of , we too wait for the birth of that , who is .  did  and  from the  of doing wrong. We celebrate the birth of  on  day.

Rebus Instructions

Use the key at the left to help with the story.

TO THE ADULT

Where activities are lectionary-based, the Sunday Scripture is noted in the green banner. Citations are from the *Lectionary for Masses with Children.*

Younger children may need help with

- The Jesse Tree, p. 2
- The Story of Advent and Christmas, p. 4
- Advent Symbols, p. 6
- Game of Love, p. 12
- Crossword Puzzle, p. 18
- Make Your Own Ornaments, p. 19
- My Gift to You, p. 25
- A Gift for Others, p. 26

Please provide children with

- crayons, markers, or colored pencils
- pencil and eraser
- glue or paste
- scissors
- construction paper
- tracing paper
- materials for the Jesse Tree

The Jesse Tree

The Jesse Tree represents Christ's family tree. Each symbol stands for an important person or event in salvation history. Cut out a Jesse Tree from construction paper, or plant an actual tree branch in a can filled with sand. Each week the class or family can remember the events of salvation history by creating and adding ornaments to the tree and talking about what the ornaments symbolize.

Every Day of Advent and Christmas

A Book of Activities for Children
Year A

C S P E C A O I
C H B B H D Z X
B E R N R V O L
E P U I I E S T
L H V L S N B C
D E H J T T K G
N R L N M Q O M
A D S T A R L A
C X Z M S G T N
C M L P Q H S G
G A L E G N A E
B R S C D Z U R
A Y J O S E P H

Advent

Christ

Christmas

Shepherd

Star

Manger

Angel

Mary

Joseph

Candle

Can You Find Them?

Find the 10 words listed above. Be sure to look carefully. They are in different directions.

_ _ _ _ _ _

TREWAH

_ _ _ _ _ _ _

DCLNEA

_ _ _ _ _ _ _ _ _ _ _

RTSA OF VDIAD

_ _ _ _

INOL

_ _ _ _ _ _ _ _ _ _ _ _

PUSTM FO SJEES

_ _ _ _

ABML

Advent Symbols

There are many important symbols during Advent. Take a minute to unscramble the words above. Then match the picture with the correct word.

Where's My Match?

Each tree is different, but there are 16 things that match. Find the matches, and connect them with lines.

O Root of Jesse

Wreath—The Second Week of Advent

We are a week closer now to our celebration of the birth of Jesus at Christmas. As you color your wreath this week, say a prayer for someone you love.

John the Baptist

Many people went out into the desert to hear John the Baptist, who was Jesus' cousin. As you color this picture, see what John had to say to the people, and think about how you, too, can prepare for the coming of Jesus.

Where Are They?

Find and circle all the animals from the manger scene. There are three sheep, a camel, a cow, and a donkey.

Connect the Dots

Enjoy what you find when you connect these dots.

Go to the

bird

Go to the

lamb

Go to the

cow

Go to the

donkey

Go to the

camel

Go to

Jesus

Place cards here

Game of Love

Cut out and shuffle the cards on the left side of this page. Place them upside down in the square to the left. Flip a coin to move. "Heads" you move two spaces, "tails" you move one space. Follow the instructions on the card, or space on the board. After you draw a card, return it to the bottom of the deck, and continue playing until someone reaches the end.

Dear Jesus

Without Jesus, we would not have Christmas. Take a minute to write a prayer or letter to Jesus. It can be about anything you choose.

DECEMBER 7

DECEMBER 8

DECEMBER 9

DECEMBER 10

DECEMBER 11

DECEMBER 12

Wreath—The Third Week of Advent

Even though we are still waiting for Jesus' coming, we rejoice today because Jesus is near. As you color the third candle the rose color of rejoicing, say a prayer for someone who brings joy into your life.

I Prepare for Jesus by Helping Others

The gospel tells us that Jesus healed and helped people. Draw onto the Jesse Tree ornaments two pictures of ways that you will help others this week.

Countdown to Christmas Calendar

Fill in your calendar! Here are 24 squares, one for each day before Christmas.

Starting with December 1, place the first square in the appropriate box. Use the calendar to help you count down to Jesus' birthday. This can be a family or individual activity.

1

5

9

10

11

15

16

17

20

21

22

2

3

4

6

7

8

12

13

14

18

19

23

24

Crossword Puzzle

During Advent, you see, hear, and feel many things. Look at the picture clues and solve the crossword puzzle.

Make Your Own Ornaments

Trace the angel and star onto tracing paper. Then trace them onto construction paper, cut them out, and decorate them on both sides. Ask an adult to help you with the hook. When you're finished, hang them on your tree or give them as gifts. Cut out and use the little gift tags in the margin for presents.

To: ____________

From: ____________

To: ____________

From: ____________

To: ____________

From: ____________

To: ____________

From: ____________

To: ____________

From: ____________

Which One Is Different?

Draw lines joining matching pairs of stars to find the one that is different from all the rest.

A Special Message

Decode this message to see what the animals are saying. (Hint: Hold this message up to a mirror, then read it!)

DECEMBER 13

DECEMBER 14

DECEMBER 15

DECEMBER 16

DECEMBER 17

DECEMBER 18

Wreath—The Fourth Week of Advent

Everywhere there are signs of getting ready for Christmas. As you color this last wreath of Advent, say this prayer:

Dear Jesus, Make my heart ready for you on Christmas. Amen

Who Is This?

Cut and paste the missing pieces together to find out who visited Joseph in a dream.

4th Sunday of Advent
Mt 1:18-24

My Decoration

Inside this ornament is a message from Jesus, whom we sometimes call "Immanuel." Starting with the first letter, read every other letter until you find the message. Fill in the blanks to reveal the message.

My Gift to You

Make your own card. Trace this Christmas card onto a piece of paper. Decorate and fold it in half. Write a special Advent or Christmas message inside.

A Gift for Others

Here is an empty gift box. Talk to an adult about what you can do to help others this Christmas. When you have given your gift, draw a picture of what you did or cut and paste the right picture inside the gift box.

The Birth of Jesus

Cut on the dotted lines and paste the missing people or objects that belong in this picture.

High upon the hills, a young shepherd watched over his flock. Then suddenly, a bright light flashed across the sky. The light was so bright that it hurt his eyes. When he looked up to the sky, he saw an angel floating in front of him. The shepherd felt very scared. The angel, with a kind and loving face, said to the shepherd, "Don't be afraid of me. I have some good news to share. God's Son is here. You must go see him. You can find the baby wrapped in cloth and lying in a manger."

My Christmas Picture

Read the story above, then create your own Christmas picture on the next page. You may wish to use crayons, markers, glue, glitter, scissors, paper, and other things you find at home or school.

Christmas
Lk 2:1-14

DECEMBER 19

DECEMBER 20

DECEMBER 21`

DECEMBER 22

DECEMBER 23

DECEMBER 24

My Christmas Picture

By: ______________________________

Christmas

Lk 2:1-14

Which Way?

The wise men heard the good news. They want to visit the new baby, but they don't know how to get there. Help them find their way.

Epiphany
Mt 2:1-12

Three Kings Match-up

On the way to see Jesus, these kings lost their things. Draw a line between each thing and the right king. (Hint: Each king is missing five things.)

O Come, Let Us Adore Him

A Picture to Color

Liguori
One Liguori Drive
Liguori MO 63057-9999

Design and illustration: Wendy Barnes, Christine Kraus, Jodi Hendrickson, and Chris Sharp.
Cover image: Getty Images/Artville

ISBN 978-0-7648-1206-4